INGRID GOFF-MAIDOFF

Andrews McMeel
Publishing, LLC

Kansas City

07 08 09 10 11 LEO 10 9 8 7 6 5 4 3 2 1

ISBN-13: 978-0-7407-7022-7
ISBN-10: 0-7407-7022-5

Library of Congress Control Number: 2007925793

www.andrewsmcmeel.com

ATTENTION: SCHOOLS AND BUSINESSES
Andrews McMeel books are available at quantity discounts with bulk purchase for educational, business, or sales promotional use. For information, please write to: Special Sales Department, Andrews McMeel Publishing, LLC, 4520 Main Street, Kansas City, Missouri 64111.

Introduction

"WORDS THAT ENLIGHTEN THE SOUL ARE MORE PRECIOUS THAN JEWELS."

—HAZRAT INAYAT KHAN

Within the wisdom of these inspirations is the message that happiness is a quality of temperament, perspective, and inner wealth. It is a blessing that each of us possesses, and rarely must pursue. In remembering the gifts we have forgotten, and giving thanks for all that we have, the clouds that sometimes block our awareness of happiness lift, and our joy and peace are restored.

Enjoy these selections on happiness as medicine for your mind, light for your soul, and a song for your heart.

May they contribute deep radiance and appreciation to living every day.

Happiness cannot be traveled to,
owned, earned, won, or consumed.
Happiness is the spiritual experience
of living every minute
with love, grace, and gratitude.

—DENIS WAITLEY

Man is unhappy because
he doesn't know he's happy.

—KIRILOV IN FYODOR DOSTOYEVSKY'S
THE POSSESSED

To fill the hour—that is happiness;
to fill the hour, and leave no crevice
for repentance or an approval.

—RALPH WALDO EMERSON

THE SECRET OF *health*
FOR BOTH MIND AND BODY
IS NOT TO MOURN FOR THE
PAST, NOR WORRY ABOUT
THE FUTURE,
BUT TO *live* THE PRESENT
MOMENT WISELY AND
EARNESTLY.

—BUDDHA

Very little is needed
to make a happy life;
it is all within yourself,
in your way of thinking.

—MARCUS AURELIUS

Sometimes simply slowing down, resting,
and tuning in to the Self
are all you need to do
to have happiness, peace, and beauty
reveal themselves to you.

—INGRID GOFF-MAIDOFF

We must bring about a revolution in our way of living our everyday lives, because our happiness, our lives, are within ourselves.

—THICH NHAT HANH

Happiness . . . leads none of us by the same route.

—CHARLES CALEB COLTON

One must never look for happiness:
one meets it by the way.

—ISABELLE EBERHARDT

A sight of happiness is happiness.

—THOMAS TRAHERNE

We have what we *seek*.
It is there all the time,
and if we *give* it time,
it will make itself
known to us.

—THOMAS MERTON

What lies behind us
    and what lies before us
are tiny matters compared to
    what lies within us.

—RALPH WALDO EMERSON

Even if happiness forgets you a little bit,
never completely forget about it.

—JACQUES PRÉVERT

Sadness is but a wall
between two gardens.

—KAHLIL GIBRAN

Live in each season

as it passes;

breathe the air,

drink the drink,

taste the fruit.

—HENRY DAVID THOREAU

The car has broken down,
my love is far away.
My bones feel weary,
and my mind is tired.
Still, I can say with joy
that happiness remains.

—INGRID GOFF-MAIDOFF

Happiness is neither virtue

nor pleasure,

not this thing or that,

but simply growth.

We are happy

when we are growing.

—WILLIAM BUTLER YEATS

DWELL AS NEAR AS POSSIBLE
TO THE CHANNEL IN WHICH
YOUR *life* FLOWS.

—HENRY DAVID THOREAU

The future belongs to those who
believe in the beauty of their dreams.

—ELEANOR ROOSEVELT

I'd rather learn from one bird
how to sing than teach ten thousand
stars how not to dance.

—E.E. CUMMINGS

THOSE WHO *wish* TO SING

ALWAYS FIND A SONG.

—SWEDISH PROVERB

When we listen
    to the still small voice within,
it is saying, "I want an earth that
    is healthy, a world at peace,
    and a heart filled with love . . .
I want my life to count."

—EKNATH ESWARAN

I have no money, no
resources, no hopes.
I am the happiest
man alive.

—HENRY MILLER

That man is richest
whose pleasures are cheapest.

—HENRY DAVID THOREAU

There is only one happiness in this life,
to love and be loved.

—GEORGE SAND

When we constructively praise
and creatively bless,
life abounds with love, peace,
     and joy.
Let goodness shine forth.

—ERNEST HOLMES

Happiness is when what you think, what you say, and what you do are in harmony.

—GANDHI

BUT WHAT IS *happiness* EXCEPT THE SIMPLE HARMONY BETWEEN A MAN AND THE *life* HE LEADS.

—ALBERT CAMUS

It is the simple things in life
that make living worthwhile,
        the sweet fundamental things
such as love and duty,
        work and rest,
and living close to nature.

—LAURA INGALLS WILDER

To love what you do and
feel that it matters—
how could anything be more fun?

—KATHERINE GRAHAM

Anticipate the good
so that you may enjoy it.

—ETHIOPIAN PROVERB

The Infinite Goodness

has such wide arms, it takes

everyone that turns to it.

—DANTE

*Know the arms of happiness
hold you as a loving mother
holds her child.*

—INGRID GOFF-MAIDOFF

Mix a little foolishness in with
your serious plans.
It is lovely to be silly at the right moment.

—HORACE

The burden of self is lightened
when I laugh at myself.

—RABINDRANATH TAGORE

CHANGE EVERYTHING—
except YOUR LOVES.

—VOLTAIRE

Be content with what you have;
rejoice in the way things are.
When you realize there is nothing lacking,
the whole world belongs to you.

—LAO TZU

Thank God for the
things I do not own.

—SAINT TERESA OF AVILA

With gratitude arises an atmosphere of happiness—a cheerful optimism. When we are grateful, we are giving attention to a world that is radiant with blessings and worthy of our notice.

—INGRID GOFF-MAIDOFF

HAPPINESS *depends* ON OURSELVES.

—ARISTOTLE

The greatest part of our happiness and misery depends on our dispositions and not on our circumstances.

—MARTHA WASHINGTON

Content makes poor men rich; Discontent makes rich men poor.

—BENJAMIN FRANKLIN

*A thankful person is thankful under
all circumstances.
A complaining soul complains even
if he lives in paradise.*

—BAHÁ'U'LLÁH

SOMETIMES YOUR *joy*
IS THE SOURCE OF YOUR SMILE,
BUT SOMETIMES YOUR *smile*
CAN BE THE SOURCE OF YOUR JOY.

—THICH NHAT HANN

THE *journey* IS THE REWARD.

—CHINESE PROVERB

May all beings everywhere
be free from suffering.
May all beings everywhere be fed.
May all beings everywhere be peaceful.
May all beings everywhere be happy.

—BUDDHIST MEDITATION

Such blessings we receive,
such gifts of grace!
If we have wandered
from the path of gladness,
point us back to life!

—INGRID GOFF-MAIDOFF

Since you get more joy
    out of giving joy to others,
you should put a great deal
    of thought into the happiness
    that you are able to give.

—ELEANOR ROOSEVELT

The big question is whether
you are going to be able to say a
hearty "yes!" to your adventure.

—JOSEPH CAMPBELL

Happiness is like a butterfly,
which, when pursued,
is always beyond your grasp,
but, which, when you sit down,
may alight upon you.

—NATHANIEL HAWTHORNE

Lost in this sad field—
startled by a butterfly.
One glimpse, and I'm found!

—INGRID GOFF-MAIDOFF

Don't search for the answers. . . .
Live the questions. . . .
Live your way into the answer. . . .

—RAINER MARIA RILKE

The butterfly counts not months but moments, and has time enough.

—RABINDRANATH TAGORE

Every situation—no, every moment—
is of infinite worth;
for it is the representative of a whole eternity.

—JOHANN WOLFGANG VON GOETHE

Eternity is a dimension
of the here and now.

—JOSEPH CAMPBELL

All moments are key moments,
and life itself is grace.

—FREDERICK BUECHNER

For everything that
lives is holy.
Life delights in life.

—WILLIAM BLAKE

Take long walks in stormy weather
or through deep snow
    in the fields and woods,
if you would keep your spirits up.
Deal with brute nature.
Be cold and hungry and weary.

—HENRY DAVID THOREAU

Human felicity is produced not so much by great pieces of good fortune that seldom happen, as by little advantages that occur every day.

—BENJAMIN FRANKLIN

ALL THE WAY TO *heaven*
IS HEAVEN.

—SAINT CATHERINE OF SIENNA

At the end of our life
our questions are simple:
Did I live fully? Did I love well?

—JACK KORNFIELD

If only we'd stop trying to be happy—
we'd have a pretty good time.

—EDITH WHARTON

BE *happy*. IT'S ONE WAY
OF BEING WISE.

—COLETTE

Thank goodness for the trash tonight.
Dragging it to the curb,
I saw the night sky filled with stars.

—INGRID GOFF-MAIDOFF

Be like the bird,
        pausing in his flight
On limb too slight,
Feels it give way, yet sings,
Knowing he has wings.

—VICTOR HUGO

You can think as much as you like,
but you will invent nothing better
than bread and salt.

—RUSSIAN PROVERB

With our thoughts
we make the world.

—BUDDHA

If you're focusing on what's good,
    what's right, what's pleasant
    and what's worth appreciating
around and within you, then
you're doing a great deal to promote
health, happiness, joy, and loving.

—JOHN-ROGER AND PETER MCWILLIAMS

Seek not happiness
too greedily,
and be not fearful
of happiness.

—LAO TZU

Take time to be friendly—
　　　　　It is the road to happiness.
Take time to dream—
　　　It is hitching your wagon to a star.
Take time to love and be loved—
　　　　　It is the privilege of the gods. . . .
Take time to look around—
　　　　　It is too short a day to be selfish.
Take time to laugh—
　　　　　It is the music of the soul.

—OLD ENGLISH BLESSING

Ten thousand flowers in spring,
the moon in autumn,
a cool breeze in summer,
snow in winter.
If your mind isn't clouded by
unnecessary things,
this is the best season of your life.

—WU-MEN

If you want others to be happy,
practice compassion.
If you want to be happy,
practice compassion.

—DALAI LAMA

Happiness comes when your work
and your words are of benefit
to yourself and others.

—BUDDHA

Write it on your heart
that every day is the
best day of the year.

—RALPH WALDO EMERSON

Go forth in every direction—
for the happiness, the harmony,
the welfare of the many.
Offer your heart,
the seeds of understanding,
like a lamp overturned and re-lit,
illuminating the darkness.

—BUDDHA

I am grateful to the many voices contributing wisdom to these pages. If they speak to you, study their lives, seek out their books, and weave what you learn into your daily living. May their words enlighten your soul. Together may we light up the world.